ON THE E AT DELPHI

Plutarch

Translated by Charles William King. Initially
Published in 1908.

"I lately, my dear Serapion, met with some little verses, that are not bad; which Dicaearchus supposes Euripides to address to Archelaus:—

"'I do not choose to offer thee a gift,
For I am poor, whilst thou art passing rich;
Else thou will either take me for a fool,
Or think that in my *giving* l am *begging*.'

For he does no favor who gives a little out of a little to those possessing much, and being suspected of not giving for no return, he incurs to boot the character of servility and meanness. In the same degree, therefore, that substantial presents fall short both in respectability and in beauty of those proceeding from reason and learning, is it a fine thing for the latter to be given, and for the giver to demand a return in kind from the receivers. For I, in sending off to you, and through you to our friends at the same place some of our Pythian conversation, in the way of first fruits, boldly confess that I expect from you in return others both longer and better done; seeing that you have the advantage of a very great city, and plenty of leisure in the midst of books and lectures of every kind. Now, our friend Apollo appears to cure and to settle all difficulties connected with life, by giving responses to such as consult him; but of himself to inspire and suggest doubts concerning what is speculative, by implanting in the knowledge-seeking part of the human soul an appetite that draws towards the truth; as is manifest from many other things, and from the dedication of the E. For this is not likely to have been done by chance, nor yet by lot only, in settling the precedence of all the letters of the alphabet before the god, did it obtain the rank of a sacred offering and object of admiration: but either those that first speculated about the god saw in it some peculiar and extraordinary virtue of its own, or else they used it as a symbol of some important mystery, and admitted it on those grounds. This question, though often propounded in the school, I had always quietly evaded and put off, until lately I was taught by my sons, uniting in entreaty with some others, visitors whom, as they were about to depart from Delphi, I could not politely divert from the point, nor excuse myself to them, anxious as they were to get some information upon the subject. Having, therefore, made them sit down about the Shrine, I began partly to investigate the matter myself, partly to put questions to them [being reminded], both by the place and by their words of what I had heard long ago (when Nero was visiting the spot), from Ammonius and others, when the same questions had been similarly started.

II. "That the god is no less a philosopher than a prophet, Ammonius proved to the satisfaction of all by adducing his titles one by one, and showing that he is 'Pythian' to such as begin to learn and to

3

inquire; 'Helius' and 'Phanaeus,' when part of the truth is already disclosed, and a glimpse thereof given; 'Ismenius,' when people have got the knowledge; and 'Leschenoieos' when they are active and enjoy that knowledge, and begin to converse and philosophize with one another. Now, since to philosophizing belongs to inquire, to wonder, and to doubt, it was natural, said he, that most parts of what related to the god should be hidden in enigmas, because they elicit discussion as to the wherefore, and information about the cause. For instance, in the case of the everlasting fire, that *pine* should be the only wood burned there, and *bayleaves* used for incense; and the fact that *two* Fates are set up here, whereas everywhere else *three* are the regular number: also the rule that no woman is allowed to approach the Oracle; and the existence of the Tripod—and all such instances, which, when brought before people that be not entirely brutish and soulless, act as baits, and draw them on to inquire, to listen, and to argue with one another. Look, too, at the maxims written up here, the 'Know thyself,' and the 'Nothing in extremes'—how many philosophical inquiries have they not excited; and what a crop of discussions has there not sprung up from them, as though from one sowing seed; and no less prolific do I think is the question now raised."

III. And when Ammonius had said this, my brother Lamprias replied: "And yet the explanation I have heard is a simple one, and very short; for they say that those Wise Men, by some denominated 'Sophists,' were really but *five*—namely, Chilon, Thales, Solon, Bias, Pittacus—for the Cleobulus Tyrant of the Lindians, and Periander the Corinthian, though they had no share either of virtue or wisdom, yet through their power, their friends, and their interest, forcibly took possession of the character, and usurped the name of the Wise Men, and sent forth and spread abroad all over Greece certain maxims and words similar to those uttered by the former, at which these being indignant, did not choose to expose their arrogance, nor to quarrel publicly for fame, and incur the hostility of persons of great power; having, therefore, held a meeting here, and conferred together, they dedicated that letter of the alphabet, which both holds the fifth place there, and also signifies the number Five, testifying to the god that they were but *Five*, and discarding and casting off the seventh and the sixth as not belonging to their number. That all this is not said at random, any one may know, from hearing those belonging to the Temple, calling the *golden* E that of Livia, wife of Caesar; the *bronze* one, that of the Athenians; whereas the original and most ancient one, wooden in material, they call the E of the Wise Men, not of *one*, but the joint offering of them all."

IV. Now Ammonius, quietly smiling, and suspecting that Lamprias was asserting an idea of his own, while he pretended it a legend and a report heard from others, upon a matter admitting of no disproval [made no reply]. But someone else of those present observed: "All this is like the nonsense which the Chaldean visitor lately talked: that there are *seven* of the letters that utter a sound of their own; *seven* stars that move in the heavens with an independent and unconnected motion of their own. For at the time spoken of, the E was from the beginning, the *second* in place of the vowels, and the Sun, after the Moon, of the planets-—now, all the Greeks, so to speak, regard Apollo as the same with the Sun. But this sort of stuff is mere idle talk. And indeed Lamprias has unwittingly stirred up the people belonging to the Temple against his argument, for what he has told us nobody at Delphi knows anything about; but all assert the common opinion and that of the guides, pretending that it is not the appearance nor the sound of the letter, but only the *name* of it that has any significance."

V. "Furthermore, as the Delphians themselves suppose, and as Nicander the priest said in his address, the letter is the vehicle and the form of the demand made to the god, and it holds the place of honor in the queries of those consulting the Oracle and asking, *If* [*ei*] they shall be victorious? *If* they shall marry? *If* it is advisable to make a voyage? *If* to turn farmer? *If* to go abroad? The god, wise as he is, sends the logicians about their business, who believe that nothing comes out of the particle *If,* and the demand that goes along with it; for the Word both conceives the questions subordinate to this particle as real things, and accepts them as such. And since inquiry is his peculiar right, in his character of prophet; and prayer to him, is a joint right in his character of god, they think that this letter represents the precatory no less than the inquiring element. For each one of such as pray begins with 'Oh, if,' and Archilochus says,

"'If I only were permitted Neobule's hand to touch!'

"And in *'eithe'* someone says the second syllable is an expletive, as in that verse of Sophron's, *'Hama teknon then dusmenea,'* and that of Homer, *'hos then kai ego son lusomenos,'* for that the precatory meaning is more than sufficiently expressed in the *'ei'.*"

VI. When Nicander had finished this—you know my companion Theon? well, he asked Ammonius if Logic was allowed free speech, after being so insulted? And when Ammonius encouraged him to speak and defend her, he began: "That the god is a very great logician, his own responses show, for it, forsooth, is the business of a logician both to invent and to solve double-senses. For as Plato said when an oracle was given commanding the doubling (squaring) the *cubical* dimensions of the altar, not the *linear*, which latter any mason could have done by simple measurement. An oracle had been given commanding the doubling the size of the altar at Delos, which is a problem requiring the utmost skill in geometry, that it was not this the god required, but that he encouraged the Greeks should study geometry. In the same way, the god by giving forth responses with double meanings promotes and establishes Logic, as being indispensable for all such as intend to understand him rightly. And if truly this bodily constitution of ours has its greatest force through Logic (Reasoning), inasmuch as it gives form to the most rational distinction, then assuredly such a conclusion as this is bound up with it, because even brute animals have a knowledge of the *being* of things, but to man alone hath Nature given the power of seeing and of judging *consequences*. For instance, that it *is* day, and *is* light, wolves, dogs, and birds understand; but that *if* it is day, it is light, no other creature understands save man alone; because he alone has the conception of *prior* and *posterior*, of appearance, and of connection, and of the relations of these things to one another; from which considerations proofs derive their most important principle. If, therefore, philosophy is busied about truth, and the light of truth is proof, and the

8

foundation of proof is connection—with good reason has the faculty that embraces and causes this, been consecrated by wise men to the god that most of all loves truth: and the god himself is a diviner, but divination is an art busied about the Future, derived from things present or past. For of no one thing is the birth without a cause, or the signification without a sense; but all things that be, follow after and are connected with those that have been, and those that will be with those that are, in a succession bringing them to pass from the beginning to the end; so he, that by a natural gift understands how to connect together, and interweave with each other their causes, the same person knows how to foretell—

"'What is, what shall be, and what was before.'

"And rightly hath Homer mentioned the Present first, and then the Future and the Past: because the reasoning comes from the things that *are*, according to the force of the connection; as for example, if this thing *is*, that thing precedes it; and conversely, if this thing *is*, that thing shall be, for what belongs to art and reasoning is the knowledge of consequences; but it is perception that gives the preconception to reason: whence, though it be indecent to say it, I will not shrink from saying *this* is the tripod of Truth, namely, Reason, which laying down as foundation the sequence of the ending to the preceding event, and then taking

9

into account the existence, crowns all with the conclusion of the proof. And the Pythian god, if he really takes delight in music, and in the voices of swans and the twangings of the lyre—what wonder is it if he embraces and loves, out of fondness for logic, this part of the Reason of which he sees philosophers making chief and most frequent use? And Hercules, though he had not yet set Prometheus free, nor conversed with sophists like Chiron and Atlas, but being yet a youth, and a thorough Boeotian, though at first he knocked down logic, and laughed the E to scorn; yet, taken at a later time, he was seen forcibly dragging away the Tripod, and fighting with the god for the possession of the art, since as he advanced in age he too became, it is likely, an excellent diviner, and at the same time, logician."

VII. And when Theon had done, Eustrophos, the Athenian, I think it was, who said to us: "You see how courageously Theon has defended Logic, all but putting on the lion's-skin for the purpose. In the same way we must count for nothing the whole lot put together, all things whatsoever, the natures and principles of men or gods, and consider this one as the leader and master of all things beautiful and precious—but we must hold our tongues, and sacrifice to this god the first fruits of his darling mathematics, because we believe that the E excels not the other vowels either in virtue, shape, or expression, but that it has been put in the post of honor as the symbol of a *number* which is great with reference to the whole and a capital one, that is the *Five*, from which the wise used to call reckoning 'counting by fives.'" This, said Eustrophos, not in joke, but because I, at that very time, was zealously applying myself to mathematics, for as he lived in the Academy, he was perhaps disposed to pay particular respect to the maxim:

"Nothing in extremes."

VIII. I therefore replied that Eustrophos solved the difficulty well by means of the Numeral. "For," I continued, "as all numeration is divided into even and odd, and as unity is common to both, in power: it being added makes the even number odd, and the odd number even: for people hold the two for the beginning of the even, and the three for that of the odd: and the five is produced when these numbers are mixed with each other; so with good cause has it obtained honor, as being the first product of the first; and has been named 'Marriage,' from the comparison of the even to the feminine, and again of the odd to the masculine. For in case of divisions into equal parts, the even number being every way parted asunder, leaves behind a receptive principle, as it were, in itself, and a space; but when the odd is treated in the same way, a middle part still survives that is productive of division; in which way it is more generative than the other, and when united thereto it prevails, but it never overcomes; for the even comes from both in no conjunction of the two, whereas the odd does in all. Furthermore, when added and joined to itself, each of the two exhibits its own distinctive property; for no even number united to an even number produces an odd one, nor goes beyond its proper allotment; because through weakness it is unproductive of offspring different from itself, and imperfect; whereas uneven numbers united with uneven numbers generate many even numbers by reason of their universally prolific nature. The other differences and properties of numbers one cannot go through with on the present occasion. The Five, therefore, the Pythagoreans denominate as 'Marriage,' as being generated through the resemblance of the odd number to the male and the even to the female, and, somewhere or other, it has been called 'Nature,' because by multiplication into itself, it finally ends in itself again; like as Nature having received what is the seed, and buried the same, produces in the meanwhile divers forms and figures, through which she moves her work on towards her end, and at last she exhibits the wheat again, and restores the beginning at the end of all; in like manner the other numbers, when they are multiplied result in different numbers through the augmentation, whereas the numbers five and six alone, taken as many times, reproduce and resuscitate themselves: for six times six becomes thirty-six, and five times five becomes five-and-twenty: and again, this is the case with the six but once, and singly; that is, when squared into itself; but the same thing happens to the number five [frequently] in the multiplication, and also, in a way peculiar to itself, in addition: for it makes either itself or the number ten, when alternately added to itself, and this is the case throughout, for the number copies the Final Cause. For as *that* Principle watches over and produces the world out of itself, and in return produces itself out of the world, as Heraclitus says:—

"'Exchanging all for fire, and fire for all,
Like goods for gold, or gold in place of goods;'

similarly the conjunction of the five with itself by its own nature generates nothing incomplete nor different in kind, but undergoes strictly defined changes; for it produces either itself or the number ten—that is, either its own property, or that which is perfect."

IX. "If, then, anyone should ask, What has this to do with Apollo? We reply: It has to do not only with him, but with Bacchus, who has no less property in Delphi than Apollo himself. We therefore hear theologians, partly in verse, partly in prose, setting forth and chanting how that the god, though by nature incorruptible and eternal, yet, as they tell, through some decree of fate, submitted to changes of condition, at one time set all Nature on fire, making all things like to all; at another time he was metamorphosed and turned into various shapes, states, and powers, in the same way as the universe now exists—but is called by the best-known of all his names. The wiser sort, cloaking their meaning from the vulgar, call the change into Fire 'Apollo,' on account of the reduction to one state, and also 'Phoebus' on account of its freedom from defilement and purity: but the condition and change of his turning and subdivision into airs and water and earth, and the production of animals and plants, they enigmatically term 'Exile' and 'Dismemberment.' They name him 'Dionysos' and 'Zagreus' and 'Nycteleos' and 'Isodi'; they also tell of certain destructions and disappearances and diseases and new births, which are riddles and fables pertaining to the aforesaid transformations: and they sing the dithyrambic song, filled with sufferings, and allusions to some change of state that brought with it wandering about and dispersion. For Aeschylus says: 'It is fitting the dithyrambus, with its confused roar, should accompany Dionysos: but Apollo, the orderly and sober paean.' The latter god they represent in pictures and images as exempt from age and youthful; but the other, under many guises and forms; and, generally, to the one they assign invariableness, order, and unmixed seriousness; whilst ascribing to the other a mingled playfulness and mischief, gravity and madness, they proclaim him 'Evius inciter of women, flourishing with frenzied honors, Dionysos!'—not wrongly taking what is the characteristic of either change. For, since the duration of the periods of such changes is not equal, but that of the one which they call 'Satiety' is the longer of the two, and that of the oracle giving the shorter, they observe the due proportion here, and during the rest of the year they employ the paean at the sacrifices; at the beginning of winter they revive the dithyramb and put a stop to the paean, and invoke the god with the former instead of the latter chant for the space of three months: which makes three to one the space of time they believe that the creation lasted compared to that of the conflagration."

X. "But this discussion has been prolonged beyond the fitting limits—it is, however, clear that they appropriate the number five to him (Apollo), sometimes taking it by itself as *Five*, sometimes as generating the number Ten out of itself, as [he does] the *World*. But with the art most acceptable to the god, namely Music, we do not think this number has anything to do: seeing that the chief business of harmony is, as one may say, connected with the notes. That these are five and no more, reason disproves if anyone unreasonably attempts to hunt out such a number upon the harp-strings, and in the holes of the flute. For all notes receive their birth in the proportions of arithmetic: and the proportion of the diatessaron is one and a third, that of the diapente one and a half, that of the diapason double; that of the diapente and diapason triple; and that of the diapason quadruple. But as to the note which the harmonists add to these, calling it the diatessaron and diapason, that goes out of the measure, it is not right for us to accept it, and comply with the irrational sense of hearing in a matter of reason, as in the case of a law. That, therefore, I may dismiss the five 'threes' of tetrachords, and the first five whether they are to be called 'tones,' 'tropes,' or 'harmonies,' according as, through tension or slackening of the strings, they are screwed up more or less, bass or sharp notes are produced—whilst the intervals are not *many*, but rather *infinite* in number—are not the melodies produced only *five*? namely, dieses, semi-tone, tone, tone and a half, double tone, and no other place in the voice, either less or greater, as defined by flatness or sharpness, can be possibly sounded."

XI. "Passing over many other instances of the same kind" (I continued), "I will adduce Plato, who says the world is one, but that if there be other worlds around this, and this be not the only one, they are five in number, and no more. Not but that, even if the world be one and only-created (as Aristotle supposes) it may in a certain sense be considered as composed and compacted out of five other worlds; for example, the one is of earth, the other of water, the third of fire, the fourth of air; the fifth element some call *heaven*, some *light*, others *aether*, others call this same thing the 'Quintessence,' to which alone of all bodies belongs by nature the revolving in a circle: and that not out of compulsion, or extraneous cause. For which reason truly having observed the five most beautiful and most perfect figures of things in nature, namely, the pyramid, the cube, the octahedron, the dodecahedron, the eikosihedron, and the duodecahedron, I have appropriately assigned each of them to a different element."

XII. "There are some philosophers who identify with those primitive elements the powers of the senses which are the same in number: they see the touch repulsive and earth-like; the taste, by means of moisture, appreciating the properties of the things tasted; whilst air being struck becomes in the hearing, voice and sound; and of the two remaining, smell, which the olfactory sense has obtained for its share, being an exhalation and generated by heat, is a fiery substance. And of sight, that is transparent with aether and light by reason of its affinity thereto, the constitution and the action are of like condition with those elements. Other sense has neither living thing, nor other nature does the world possess, that is simple and unmixed; but there has been made, to all appearance, a certain wonderful distribution and acceptance of the one five between the other five."

XIII. At the same moment, as it were checking myself, and leaving off, I exclaimed: "What have we been thinking of, Eustrophos, to have all but passed over Homer, as though not the first to divide the world into five portions? The three intermediate he has assigned to the three gods, the two extremes, Olympus and Earth, whereof the one is the boundary of things below, the other of things above, he has left common to all and unallotted to any. But 'the argument must be carried back,' as Euripides saith, for they that venerate the number Four do not ill to teach that by reason of this number every body has its origin. For since every thing that is solid consists in length and breadth admitting of depth; and before length exists a point set down in the way of unity; and as length is called a line without breadth, and *is* length: and the motion of a line in the direction of width gives origin to surface in the number three; and when depth is added to all these in four ways, the aggregate advances into a solid body—it is clear to everyone that the number four, after having carried Nature forward up to completing a body and producing [double] bulk and resistance, has yet left it deficient in the most important article. For the thing inanimate, to speak generally, is helpless, imperfect, and serviceable for nothing at all, without a soul to direct it; but the motion or disposition, being a change produced in five different ways, generates therein a soul, imparts perfection to its nature, and possesses a value superior to the number four, in the same degree that the living thing surpasses the thing without life. Furthermore, the proportion and force of the number five, being the more powerful, hath not suffered animate nature to run off into infinite varieties, but hath produced five species only of things animate: for there are gods (I suppose), and daemons, and heroes, and the fourth kind of men; and then the irrational and brute creation. Again, if you divide the soul itself according to its constitution, the first and darkest part of it is the nutritive, the second the sensitive, the third the appetitive, the next to this the irascible, and having arrived at the faculty of reason, and completed its nature, it takes its rest in the fifth principle as upon the highest point."

XIV. "And whilst the number possesses so many and such great virtues, its origin is likewise beautiful; not being that which we have lately discussed, springing out of the two; but what the beginning of the odd, coupling itself with the square, produces. For the beginning of all numbers is unity; and the first square is the four; and out of these as from a pattern or material having a limit, comes the five. But if, indeed, some are right in supposing the unit the first square number, being a power in itself and producing the same out of itself—in that case also the five, as generated out of the first two squares, has not lost its highest place of nobility."

XV. "But the main point," I continued, "I fear if enounced will press hard upon our friend Plato, in the same way as he himself used to say that Anaxagoras was pressed hard by the name of the Moon, when he appropriated some very ancient notion amongst those current respecting her illuminations (phases); has he not said this in the Cratylus?" "Yes, certainly," replied Eustrophos, "but what similarity there is in the present case I do not perceive." "And yet," said I, "you surely know that in the 'Sophist' he makes out the most important principles to he five in number, namely, Being, Sameness, Diversity, and fourthly and fifthly, after these, Motion and Rest. But in the ' Philebus' he uses a different mode of division, and says that *One* is infinite and *Other* definite, and that all generation is composed from these two mixed together: and the Cause by which they are so mixed together he supposes the fourth kind; whilst the fifth he leaves us to conceive as that through which the two mixed principles again obtain separation and division. But I conjecture that these things are predicated as being *images* of those ideas just mentioned, that which is born being the image of that which *is*, the infinite that of *Motion*, the finite that of *Rest*; *Sameness* being the mixing principle, *Diversity* that which separates. And if these are otherwise, even on that supposition, they will similarly be classed in five kinds and differences. Some one, forsooth, previous to Plato had put the question [to the

Oracle] and had learned this fact, and therefore dedicated two E's to the god, as an indication and symbol of the number of the all. But again, the same person may have done so because he had discovered that the Good is imagined [as being manifested] five kinds—whereof the first is what is moderate, the second what is consistent, the third Mind, the fourth the sciences, arts, and true conceptions dwelling in the soul; the fifth kind, whatever pleasure is pure and unalloyed with pain." Here he ceased, quoting the line of Orpheus:—

"'In the sixth period still the rage of song.'"

XVI. After the discourse aforesaid, he continued to us: "One thing more, briefly, I will sing to the intelligent, like Nicander and his friends. On the sixth day of the new moon, when you conduct the Pythia to the Townhall, the first casting of the three lots takes place. . . you throw neither three nor two—is it not so?" "It is so," replied Nicander; "but the reason must not be divulged to others." "Consequently," I said, smiling, "so far as the god allows us that be [not] sanctified to know the truth, this rule also has something to do with what has been said on the subject of the number five. So the list of the arithmetical and mathematical praises of the letter E, as far as I recollect then, is now concluded."

XVII. Ammonius,inasmuch as he was one who held that by no means the least important part of philosophy lay in mathematics, was delighted with what had been said, and remarked, "To argue very critically against all this is not fitting for us beginners: yet each one of the numbers taken by itself will furnish much scope for such as wish to praise it. And what need is there to talk about the others, when the Seven, sacred to Apollo, will alone exhaust the whole day, should one attempt to enumerate all its properties? In the next place, we shall prove that the Wise Men quarrelled with common custom as well as with long tradition, when they pushed down the Seven from its place of honor and dedicated the Five unto the god as the more properly pertaining to him. Neither number, therefore, nor rank, nor conjunction, nor any other of the remaining parts of speech, I think, does the letter signify, but that it is an *address* to the god, or an *invocation*, complete in itself, that together with the utterance thereof puts the speaker in mind of the power of the deity. For the god addresses each one of us here, when approaching him, as if with a salutation, in the words, 'Know thyself,' which is neither more nor less than 'Hail,' whilst we, in requital to the god, say, 'Thou art,' as though paying to him the true, undying, and sole property of himself, the predicate of *existence*."

XVIII. "For we ourselves have in reality no part in existence; for all mortal nature being in a state between birth and dissolution, presents no more than an illusion, and a semblance, shapeless and unstable of itself, and if you will closely apply your thought, out of the wish to seize hold of the idea, just as the too strong grasping at water when it is pressed together and condensed, loses it, for it slips through your fingers, in the same way Reason, in pursuing after the *appearances*, so extremely clear as they look, of each one of the conditions of life as they pass along, misses its aim; impinging on the one side against its coming into existence, on the other, against its going out; without ever laying hold upon it as a permanent thing, or as being in reality a power. It is not possible, according to Heraclitus, to step into the *same* river twice; neither is it to lay hold of mortal life twice, in the same condition; but by reason of the suddenness and speed of its mutation, it disperses and again brings together, or rather, neither *again* nor *afterwards*, but at one and the same time it subsists and it comes to an end; it approaches and it departs, wherefore it never ripens that of it which is born into actual being, by reason that Birth doth never cease nor stand still, but *transforms*; and out of the seed makes the embryo, then the child, then the youth, young man, full-grown man, elderly man, old man—obliterating the former growths and ages by those growing up over them. But we ridiculously fear *one* death, although we have already died, and are still dying, so many; for not only, as Heraclitus says, 'When fire dies is the birth of air, and when air dies is the birth of water,' but still more plainly may you see it from ourselves: the full-grown man perishes when the old man is produced, the youth had before perished into the full-grown man, and the child into the youth, and the infant into the child; and the 'yesterday' has died into the 'to-day,' and the 'to-day' is dying into the 'to-morrow,' and no one remains, nor is *one*, but we grow up many around one appearance and common model, whilst matter revolves around and slips away. Else how is it, if we remain the same, that we take pleasure in some things *now*, in different things *before*; we love contrary objects, we admire and find fault with them, we use others words, feel other passions; not having either appearance, figure, nor disposition the same as before? To be in different states, without a change, is not a possible thing, and he that is *changed* is not the *same* person; but if he is not the same, he does not exist . . . this very thing (time change) he changes——growing one different person out of another; but Sense, through ignorance of reality, falsely pronounces that what appears *exists*."

XIX. "What then is really existing? The answer is, the eternal, unborn, undecaying, to which no length of time brings about a change: for Time is a thing movable and making move, making its appearance conjointly with matter; leaking and not holding water, as it were, a vessel full of decay and growth; for is not the predicate 'After' and 'Before,' 'Future,' and 'Past,' of itself an acknowledgment of non-existence? For to say that what has not yet been, or what has ceased from being, *is* in being, how silly and absurd! For in this way especially do we apply the notion of Time, and predicate the terms 'Instant' and 'Present' and 'Now' . . . this, in turn, Reason distributes too much, dissolves and destroys. For it (Time) is diverted, like a ray of light, into the Future and the Past, necessarily separated, when we attempt to see it. And if the Nature that is measured is in the same condition as that which measures it, nothing is either stable or existing, but all things are either being born or perishing, according to their distribution with respect to time. Consequently it is not allowable so much as to say of Being that 'it was' or that 'it will be;' for all these modes are tenses, transitions, and interchanges of the thing formed by nature, never to stand still in existence.

XX. "But the god *is*, we must declare; and *is* with reference to no time, but with reference to the eternal, the immovable, timeless, and indeclinable; that which there is nothing before nor after, nor more, nor past, nor older nor younger, but He being *One* with the one 'Now,' hath filled up the 'Ever;' and that which really *is*, alone *is* with reference to Him; neither born, nor about to *be*, nor growing, nor to have an end. In this way, therefore, ought we, when worshipping, to salute Him, and to address Him, or even, truly, as some of the ancients did, 'Thou art One!' For the Deity is not *several*, as each one of us is, made up out of an infinite number of different things in conditions of existence—a motley assemblage of articles of all sorts and gleanings. But that which *is* must necessarily be *One*, just as *One* must be that which is; for difference of that which is, springs out of that which is not, in form of births, consequently the first of the names (by which he is called) well suits the god, as also the second and the third. For 'Apollo,' inasmuch as it means 'denying many,' signifies also 'rejecting plurality.'" He is also *'letos,'* because *one* and alone. 'Phoebus' the ancients called everything clean and chaste, and even now the Thessalians say that their priests, when living by themselves outside the city on the fast-days, 'are living Phoebus.' But the One is single and pure, for the mixing of one thing with another constitutes pollution; as Homer somewhere calls ivory turned purple by a dye 'polluted,' and dyers call the running together of colors 'being spoilt,' and such mixture they term 'corruption.' Hence, to be one and always unmixed belongs to the Immortal and the Pure.

XXI. "But those who hold Apollo and the Sun for one and the same, we ought to welcome and love for the omen's sake, because they embody the idea of the god in the thing which they most honor of all the objects that they know and long for. As though, therefore, they were dreaming about the god in the most beautiful of dreams, let us wake them up, and exhort them to carry their thoughts yet higher, and contemplate what is above them, and the essence; to honor indeed the *Type*, and venerate the creative force residing therein, as that which converts the Intelligible into the Sensible, and the Permanent into the Transitory—the type that shows forth in some way or other glimpses and images of the benevolence and felicity that dwell around that god. But as for his migrations and changes which bind him together when he emits fire, as they tell, and again quenches it, and directs it upon earth, sea, the winds, animals; and the dreadful sufferings of plants and living things, all such it is impiety even to hear mentioned. Otherwise the Deity would be worse than the child in the poem, as to the game it plays with a heap of sand, first built up and then thrown over: He would be playing the same game with the universe and the world; first making things that are not, then destroying what is made. For, on the contrary, whatever has been generated, in whatever way, in the world, *this* binds all existence together, and checks the infirmity inherent in the medley that tends to destruction. And to me what seems most opposed to, and testifying against the aforesaid legend is this very word, the addressing 'Thou art' to the god, as though neither change of place or transformation were possible with respect to *him*, but are applied to some other god (or better say daemon) appointed to preside over Nature as working in production and dissolution, to whom it pertained to do and suffer such things, as is evident at first sight from our god's titles, so contrary and contradictory to such a conception of his character. For the one is called Apollo, the other Pluto; the one is styled Delius (*apparent*), the other Aidoneus (*invisible*); the one Phoeleus (*bright*), the other Scotios (*full of darkness*); and by the side of the one stand the Muses and Memory, beside the other Oblivion and Silence; the one is entitled from completion and giving light, the other is the 'lord of unseeing Night and unworking Sleep;' the one is 'of all the gods most hateful to mankind,' touching whom Pindar hath said, not unpleasantly, 'He hath been condemned to be the most undelightful unto mortals.' With good cause, then, Euripides says,

**"'Drink offerings to the dead and gone,
Chants that the god with golden hair,
Phoebus, receiveth not.'**

and, before him, Sophocles, 'Above all things, sports and songs doth Apollo love; but mourning and groans Pluto hath gotten for his share.' Sophocles also has distinctly assigned to each of them his proper instruments in these words,

"'Neither the mournful flute, nor merry lyre.'

For it was late and only yesterday that the flute gave forth its sound at scenes of merriment; in old times it drawled out in lamentations, at funerals, and held this office (not a very respectable or cheerful one) at scenes of the kind. Afterwards, however, it was admitted to everything. But, to say the truth, those who have mixed up things relating to gods with those relating to daemons, have brought themselves chiefly into trouble. But indeed the maxim, 'Know thyself' appears to run counter to the 'Thou art,' and again, in one way, to harmonize with it; for the one is addressed through awe and veneration to the god, the other is a reminder to mortality of the nature and frailty that envelopes it."

Made in the USA
Las Vegas, NV
23 February 2025